THE ONE GOD DOCTRINE

Affirming the Strict Monotheism of the Scriptures

Paul Thomas

ISBN: 978-1-4717-5099-1

Contents

1. ONE GOD IN CREATION............4

2. GOD IS THE WORD.................. 23

3. GOD ALONE CAN SAVE.............42

4. ONE GOD IS THE SPIRIT......... 66

5. ONE GOD RETURNS............. 79

1. ONE GOD IN CREATION

Genesis 1:1 *In the beginning God created the Heaven and the earth.*

The Bible begins with the introduction of God as the Creator of the Heavens and the earth. He is presented as "God" – one individual. 2883 times do we find the phrase, "And God…" but we never find, "And Gods…" in reference to the holy God of the Bible. This is the first evidence that the God of the Bible is one without *any divisions.*

We have further evidence that He is strictly one, in that He spoke as one individual. This is confirmed by the declaration, "And God *said…*" (Genesis 1:3). It is one God who conceived of the Creation and spoke it unilaterally into existence. There are those who believe that three persons in the Godhead consult lovingly with each other and agree to work in harmony, much like a committee. This understanding is not supported by Scripture.

> ***Isaiah 40:14*** *With whom took he counsel, and who instructed him, and taught him in the path of judgment, and taught him knowledge, and shewed to him the way of understanding?*

Christians affirm that God is almighty and all-powerful. However, for this to be true, we should demonstrate that He is (a) by Himself, and (b) accomplishes the act of Creation *alone*. To suggest that God is a triune being negates both points because three persons or beings are not almighty or all-powerful simply because they are dependent on each other to accomplish the creative act. The God of the Bible makes it crystal clear that He accomplished the act of Creation alone and by Himself.

> ***Isaiah 44:24*** *Thus saith the Lord, thy redeemer, and he that formed thee from the womb, I am the Lord that maketh all things; that stretcheth forth the Heavens alone; that spreadeth abroad the earth by myself;*

By stating that He was *alone* in the act of Creation, God is ruling out any collaborative act involving a plurality of beings/persons. In addition, *by myself* serves to reinforce the fact that Creation is a task accomplished by this one God, alone. *By myself* indicates that God began and finished the work, assisted by none, which is why one of His favorite titles is the "first and the last."

> ***Isaiah 44:6*** *Thus saith the Lord the King of Israel, and his redeemer the Lord of hosts; I am the first, and I am the last; and beside me there is no God.*

Think about it for a moment: given the monumental task of Creation, would God not desire to credit any other person/being if He did, indeed, receive some input from them in the act of Creation? We believe, given His holy and moral nature, that He indeed would have. On the contrary, however, we find that God repeatedly denies the involvement of any other person/being in Creation. Trinitarians strongly believe that denial of the personhood of each member of the Trinity is heresy. Why, then, does Scripture not credit, even in passing, the role of each of these "persons" in bringing about the existence of the world? Why are we told on several occasions that one God created the world? Take Malachi, for instance:

> ***Malachi 2:10*** *Have we not all one father? hath not one God created us? why do we deal treacherously every man against his brother, by profaning the covenant of our fathers?*

Malachi's question is rhetorical. He was just declaring what all of Israel believed. It was this holy belief in the one God which made Israel unique in every way. The surrounding nations were saturated with a multiplicity of gods, and to them, the creed of Israel was revolutionary. God took Israel out of Egypt and into the Land of Canaan so she could freely profess this creed. The enemy of truth, Satan, was so afraid of the power of believing in one God that he wasted no time in seducing Israel to worship other gods *right at the foot of Mount Sinai.*

> ***Exodus 32:7*** *And the Lord said unto Moses, Go, get thee down; for thy people, which thou broughtest out of the land of Egypt,*

> ***Exodus 32:8*** *They have turned aside quickly out of the way which I commanded them: they have made them a molten calf, and have worshipped it, and have sacrificed thereunto, and said, These be thy gods, O Israel, which have*

brought thee up out of the land of Egypt. have corrupted themselves:

Why was Satan so afraid? It was because Moses was, at the same instant, receiving the commandment which would, from then on, shake his kingdom of darkness. This holy commandment, "Thou shalt have no other gods before me," (Exodus 20:3) was accompanied with lightning, thunder, fire, and smoke. It strikes terror into the forces of darkness. Anyone who embraces this simple truth will be delivered from the bondage of the evil one. Remember what James says:

> ***James 2:19*** *Thou believest that there is one God; thou doest well: the devils also believe, and tremble.*

Where God is acknowledged in His true essence – as the one and only God – His Spirit takes up residence. On the other hand, where the one God doctrine is compromised, the presence of God leaves. I have lived in India for over 10 years. In addition, I was a short-term missionary there, in 2002-2003. Few other countries in the world are as given over to idol-worship as India. There are countless gods and goddesses, with millions of followers (devotees) in every corner of the land. Besides the three main gods – Brahma (the creator), Vishnu (the preserver), and Shiva (the destroyer) – there are local deities, each associated with a particular area. I am convinced that much of the grinding poverty, diseases, social divisions (e.g. the caste system), and endemic corruption is due to the sin against the one God doctrine. A nation pays a very high price for corrupting the holy doctrine of the one God, as Israel found out when God rejected them and gave them over to the Assyrians in 721 B.C.

> ***2 Kings 17:9*** *And the children of Israel did secretly those things that were not right against the Lord their God, and they built them high places in all their cities, from the tower of the watchmen to the fenced city.*

> ***2 Kings 17:10*** *And they set them up images and groves in every high hill, and under every green tree:*

> ***2 Kings 17:20*** *And the* LORD *rejected all the seed of Israel, and afflicted them, and delivered*

them into the hand of spoilers, until he had cast them out of his sight.

In the pages of the Bible, God uses the first person singular pronoun "I" in speaking of His creative act.

> ***Job 38:4*** *Where wast thou when I laid the foundations of the earth? declare, if thou hast understanding.*

This underscores the point that He was the sole architect and implementer of the act of Creation. The word "I" is not susceptible to any divisions or multiplicities. If a human being were to say "I," we take it for granted that the speaker speaks as one, single, integrated and conscious person/being, unless mentally compromised. It goes without saying that the "I" of God must be accorded the same respect.

Some Trinitarians expect us to understand the "I" as the collective "I" of all three persons in a triune Godhead. This raises serious questions about the notion of personhood and individuality. If all three persons are saying "I," then there is a question about the authenticity of each one's personhood. In other words, all three persons saying "I" blurs the distinction of their personhood – their individual personalities are merged to such a degree that it makes little or no sense to say "I". What we are faced with is an unexamined use of language with reference to God. It was Ludwig Wittgenstein who stated that words have no meaning outside of the "language games" we humans construct and play by. In other words, if we learned the meaning of "I" by observing someone pointing to themselves, then a child is socialized to understand that "I" refers to a single individual. In this sense, Trinitarians employ words in a way which contravenes common usage or "language games," as Wittgenstein would have put.

With regards to the number of persons or entities involved in the Creation of the world, the Bible is consistently clear – one God. The verse below reiterates this truth.

> ***Isaiah 45:18*** *For thus saith the Lord that created the Heavens; God himself that formed the earth and made it; he hath established it, he*

> *created it not in vain, he formed it to be inhabited: I am the Lord; and there is none else.*

As will be shown later, this same God was manifested in the flesh (I Timothy 3:16). This means that Jesus is not another God, or a second member of the Trinity, but the very same Jehovah of the Old Testament who robed Himself in flesh. It is for this reason that John declares Jesus to be the Creator of everything. In fact, John sates that all things were made by *him*:

> ***John 1:3*** *All things were made by him; and without him was not any thing made that was made.*

Not only is Jesus identified as the Creator, but John uses the third person singular objective pronoun *Him,* which, again, is not susceptible to further divisions. In a similar vein, the Apostle Paul, who spent much of his energy and time fighting against what he saw as blasphemy – that Jesus is God – himself identifies Jesus as the one Creator of everything in existence in the universe.

Colossians 1:16 *For by him were all things created, that are in Heaven, and that are in earth, visible and invisible, whether they be thrones, or dominions, or principalities, or powers: all things were created by him, and for him:*

"For by him…" rules out any suggestion that there was more than one God behind the creative work. Thus we observe over and over again that, in relation to the Creation of all things, the Bible uses language such as, *one God, he, him, himself, alone,* and *myself* overwhelmingly. As mentioned earlier, this is not a marginal issue; on the contrary, it goes to the very heart of what we mean by God being Almighty. Only one God can lay claim to being almighty and omnipotent (having all power). And where else, but in the act of Creation should we expect this to be true?

It would be a scandal if a great architect, like Sir Christopher Wren (1632-1723), was not recognized for a masterpiece, such as St .Paul's Cathedral in London. How much more, if we are not told who or how many individuals were responsible for the Creation of the universe? We owe our very existence to this being and would want to thank and worship Him as the Scriptures decree.

> ***Matthew 4:10*** *Then saith Jesus unto him, Get thee hence, Satan: for it is written, Thou shalt worship the Lord thy God, and him only shalt thou serve.*

Notice again, that Jesus uses language which cannot be misunderstood: "Thou shalt worship **the Lord**…and **Him only**…" Because this language is so clear, I am convinced that those who insist in sharing the glory of this one God with a diffuse Trinity or committee must answer to this Judge, whom they will see sitting on **one** throne in Heaven.

> ***Revelation 4:2*** *And immediately I was in the spirit: and, behold, a throne was set in Heaven, and one sat on the throne.*

Why is it essential to believe that the God of the Bible is one, in a strict monotheistic sense? It is because we are commanded to love this God with all our heart, soul, might, and mind (Deuteronomy 6:4 & Mark 12:30). A human is created with one heart, mind, and soul. This logically means that we are made to make only one God the object of our total love, attention, dedication, and worship. I once read the story of a Muslim woman who converted to Christianity, and then reverted back to Islam. She stated that she found it impossible to give equal attention to three persons in the Godhead. She was nagged by the guilt of ignoring one or the other of the members of the Trinity when she prayed. It is my heartfelt prayer that individuals who struggle with such issues, unrelated to the Bible, will read booklets like this and take heart. In Heaven, the 24 elders gave praise to *one God, alone*, for the Creation of all things, for which they showered Him with adoration. Scripture is saturated with all of the earlier ingredients of the doctrine of one God. Can anyone doubt that God is singularly one in the Creation?

> ***Revelation 4:11*** *Thou art worthy, O Lord, to receive glory and honour and power: for thou hast created all things, and for thy pleasure they are and were created.*

How did others in the Bible understand the Godhead in Creation? Nehemiah, for example, was a competent administrator and exegete of the Word of God. We remember how he, among others, cleansed the Temple, rebuilt the walls of Jerusalem, restored the Levites, and always sought to correctly interpret and implement the Law of Moses. Gripped by a spirit of worship, he glorified the one God who not only created all things, but sustains it. Again, we note the language which is free of any subtle, covert or overt connotation of plurality.

> ***Nehemiah 9:6*** *Thou, even thou, art Lord alone; thou hast made Heaven, the Heaven of Heavens, with all their host, the earth, and all things that are therein, the seas, and all that is therein, and thou preservest them all; and the host of Heaven worshippeth thee.*

The Bible gives us a simple rule for determining the validity of a teaching: there must be two or three witnesses (Deuteronomy 17:6). We are exhorted to search from the book of the Lord and establish a truth by linking a verse with another. In the words of Isaiah, "none shall want her mate" (Isaiah 34:16). Take a look at the verse, below. It almost seems to contain the same language and understanding as Nehemiah 9:6. Notice how both verses stress "alone".

> ***2 Kings 19:15*** *And Hezekiah prayed before the Lord, and said, O Lord God of Israel, which dwellest between the cherubims, thou art the God, even thou alone, of all the kingdoms of the earth; thou hast made Heaven and earth.*

I will now address one verse of Scripture which has frequently been used to argue for a plurality of beings in the Godhead. In the verse below, some take the "us" as evidence of a plurality, and hence, a Trinity.

> ***Genesis 1:26*** *And God said, Let us make man in our image, after our likeness: and let them have dominion over the fish of the sea, and over the fowl of the air, and over the cattle, and over all the earth, and over every creeping thing that creepeth upon the earth.*

Before we proceed, it is vital to underscore that one cannot find "evidence" for the doctrine of the Trinity in Genesis 1:26. "Us" can be any number between two and infinity. Even the charismatic preacher, Benny Hinn, ran into trouble when he once publicly declared that there are nine in the

Trinity. To argue convincingly for the Trinity, one must demonstrate the existence of only 3 persons, who somehow are simultaneously one. Any objective person can see that there is no room for developing such a theory in Genesis 1:26.

To properly understand Genesis 1:26, we need to first look at the next verse, as sound Bible hermeneutics dictates.

> ***Genesis 1:27*** *So God created man in his own image, in the image of God created he him; male and female created he them.*

What was the result of the Creation of man? How many men arose from the dust? The answer is one because God made man in *his own image.* Had God existed as a triune being (an "us"), we should expect 3 persons, or one man who is at the same time three persons, taking form out of the dust. In other words, the fact that a human being is one indivisible person is tangible proof that God is indivisibly one. Another lesson we can draw from Genesis 1:27 is that the writer states, "male and female created he *them.*" Observe how careful he is to differentiate between God as *he* and the first couple as *them*. Surely the writer would have let us know plainly if God was a triune being. If the doctrine of the Trinity is vital to salvation – as many Christians maintain – why is it not plainly declared from the outset of the Bible? Why was it left to men who came almost 2000 years later to understand and develop this theology? And what about the Israelites themselves? Are we to conclude that they not only missed out on the identity of their Messiah, but also were in the dark about the true nature of the one God they claimed to serve all along?

Returning to Genesis 1:26, the clue lies in the Hebrew for "us" which is *Elohim*. Elohim is indeed in the plural form, but is often used to refer to a single person. Here is an example:

> ***Exodus 7:1*** *And the Lord said unto Moses, See, I have made thee a god to Pharaoh: and Aaron thy brother shall be thy prophet.*

God made Moses an *Elohim* to Pharaoh. The exact word for "us" in Genesis 1:26 is also used in the case of Moses. Despite this, we do not conclude that Moses is a triune being. Why do we not apply the same standard to both Scriptures? What God was saying is that Moses would be a judge to Pharaoh, and not a divine being. This demonstrates the fact that a single individual can be addressed as *Elohim,* although the word is in the plural form. The Greek scholar, Spiros Zodhiates[1], concludes, with respect to "us" in Genesis 1:26, "It usually takes a singular verb, so no implication of any plurality in the divine nature can be inferred from the fact that the word is plural" (Zodhiates, 1984, p. 1578). What this means is that we will not find phrases where *Elohim* is followed by a plural verb, e.g. Elohim *are*… which proves that *Elohim* (us) is singular and buttresses the one God doctrine. In fact, we find other places in the Bible where single individuals have referred to themselves as "us". Daniel the prophet was one man, and yet he speaks of himself employing the plural "we".

1

Zodhiates, S. (1984). *Hebrew-Greek Key Study Bible* (Third printing ed.). Chattanooga: AMG Publisher International, Inc.

> ***Daniel 2:19*** *Then was the secret revealed unto Daniel in a night vision. Then Daniel blessed the God of Heaven.*

> ***Daniel 2:36*** *This is the dream; and we will tell the interpretation thereof before the king.*

Another strong argument for the doctrine of the one, indivisible God in the act of Creation are the words of the Lord Jesus Christ Himself.

> ***Matthew 19:4*** *And he answered and said unto them, Have ye not read, that he which made them at the beginning made them male and female,*

The Lord Jesus Christ declares authoritatively that *he* made them in the beginning male and female. He must mean just that – He. It is not possible to philosophize this simple truth away. The God who made the first couple is called *He.* Let us be content to accept this revelation from the mouth of He who made all things (John 1:3).

Finally, the Bible tells us that the one God, who addresses Himself as "I," will create a new Heaven and a new earth.

> ***Revelation 21:5*** *And he that sat upon the throne said, Behold, I make all things new. And he said unto me, Write: for these words are true and faithful.*

In the final analysis of the doctrine of one God in Creation, we come back full circle – the same one God creates all things anew at the end of age. This chapter has shown, especially through the writings of the prophet Isaiah, that God claims to be by Himself and alone in the act of Creation. Jesus reprimanded the Jews for not listening to Isaiah, accusing them of hypocrisy and teaching for doctrine the traditions of men (Matthew 15:7-9). I pray that you, the reader, will humbly embrace the message of Isaiah – that God is alone and by Himself in Creation. Let the plain sense of Scripture be the best rule of interpretation.

In the next chapter, I will focus on the manner in which the Word of God is identical with God Himself, and does not constitute a distinct person.

2. GOD IS THE WORD

The children of Israel have always believed that the Word of God is identical with God. They never entertained any ideas of a distinction or separation between God and His Word. Whatever could be said of God could be said about His Word. Just as a human being is known by his or her words, God also expressed Himself by His Word. The very first such self-expression was in the Garden of Eden.

> ***Genesis 3:8*** *And they heard the voice of the Lord God walking in the garden in the cool of the day: and Adam and his wife hid themselves from the presence of the Lord God amongst the trees of the garden.*

For some reason, I had for years overlooked what this Scripture was really saying…*they heard the voice of the Lord God walking…* How does someone's voice walk? One reason we find this baffling is because we do not associate intangible personal characteristics, like voices or thoughts, with physical actions. Note that Genesis 3:8 is not metaphorical because Adam and Eve hid themselves from the presence of the Lord. The voice of God walked and His walking was heard by Adam and Eve. There is only one conclusion to draw: God and His Word are indistinguishable; His Word is He, Himself, and He Himself is His very own Word. The Word of God is His creative, expressive power. It is creative because, by it, He creates new and amazing things. The Word of God is expressive because, through it, He declares Himself and makes His identity known. It was through His voice or Word that He sought fellowship with Adam and Eve so He could make Himself known to them.

Sometime later, when the time had come to declare Himself to the children of Israel, God made Himself know by His Word, again.

> **Deuteronomy 4:10** *Specially the day that thou stoodest before the Lord thy God in Horeb, when the Lord said unto me, Gather me the people together, and I will make them hear my words, that they may learn to fear me all the days that they shall live upon the earth, and that they may teach their children.*

> ***Deutereonomy 4:12*** *And the Lord spake unto you out of the midst of the fire: ye heard the voice of the words, but saw no similitude; only ye heard a voice.*

The only permissible way in which we can know the God of the Bible is through His Word. His Word reveals His identity, His character, and His attributes. Since absolutely nothing we know of, or can conceive of, can encapsulate the great glory of God, we are forbidden to fashion any idols or imagine His being except, through His revealed Word (Deuteronomy 4:15-19).

In the last chapter, we saw how the Scriptures clearly testify that God, alone, created all things. How did He go about creating all things? The answer is through His Word, which is His expressive, creative power. Simply put, God creates through His Word. This Word is, to emphasize once more, not another individual or divine being with his own consciousness, but the very same God.

> ***Psalm 33:6*** *By the word of the Lord were the Heavens made; and all the host of them by the breath of his mouth.*

Just consider the power and effect of our own words. Our words can edify, soothe, excite, refresh, or discourage, provoke, and bore. If we have the power to trigger such emotions - which sometimes have serious consequences - how much more the Word of God? A person is known by his or her words, whether they are gentle, intelligent, humble, or crass, dim, and proud. God's Word, too, reveals not only His power, but His character. Interestingly, the verse, below, equates the appearance of God with the revelation of His Word to the child prophet, Samuel.

> ***1Samuel 3:21*** *And the Lord appeared again in Shiloh: for the Lord revealed himself to Samuel in Shiloh by the word of the Lord.*

Put differently, a person who receives the understanding or revelation of the Word of God, as revealed in the Bible, can say that God appeared to him. Perhaps, this is hard for us humans to grasp, and even more difficult to accept. We often ask the Lord to appear physically to us because we are sight-oriented: "seeing is believing" is a popular aphorism. This is when we need to remind ourselves of the words of our Lord Jesus Christ.

> ***John 20:29*** *Jesus saith unto him, Thomas, because thou hast seen me, thou hast believed: blessed are they that have not seen, and yet have believed.*

The history of God's dealings with the children of Israel demonstrates that seeing may be overrated. They saw countless miracles, but remained in unbelief, for which they could not enter the Promised Land. Why is this? Perhaps, it has something to do with the fact that our brains play games with us, telling us that we did not see what was plainly evident. In addition, Satan can work miracles; thus, deceiving those who witness them. "Even him, whose coming is after the working of Satan with all power and signs and lying wonders," (2 Thessalonians 2:9). It is for these reasons that God always revealed Himself through His Word to His holy prophets.

> **Genesis 15:1** *After these things the word of the Lord came unto Abram in a vision, saying, Fear not, Abram: I am thy shield, and thy exceeding great reward.*

2Samuel 7:4 *And it came to pass that night, that the word of the Lord came unto Nathan, saying,*

1Kings 21:17 *And the word of the Lord came to Elijah the Tishbite, saying,*

Jeremiah 1:11 *Moreover the word of the Lord came unto me, saying, Jeremiah, what seest thou? And I said, I see a rod of an almond tree.*

All the above verses confirm the truth that the coming of the Word of God is the same as His appearance to an individual. When a prophet was inspired to speak in the name of the Lord, the Lord, Himself, took up position, if you will, in the prophet, filled his spirit with His presence, and expressed Himself through the vocal chords and tongue of the prophet. Often, they had no idea what they were saying because, as Peter declares, they were ministering to the saints of the Church in the future.

1 Peter 1:12 *Unto whom it was revealed, that not unto themselves, but unto us they did minister the things, which are now reported unto you by them that have preached the gospel unto you with* *the Holy Ghost sent down from Heaven; which things the angels desire to look into.*

It was gentile philosophers, like Justin Martyr (AD 100-165), who were responsible for speculating that the Word of God and God are not identical. In effect, he put a wedge between God and His Word, ultimately inventing a new god.

> *For next to God, we worship and love the Logos who is out of the unbegotten and ineffable God, since also He became man for our sakes, that, becoming a partaker of our sufferings, He might also bring us healing (Second Apology, 13).*

> *There is, and that there is said to be, another God and Lord subject to the Maker of all things who is also called an Angel, because He announces to men whatsoever the Maker of all things, above whom there is no other God, wishes to announce to them.... I shall endeavour to persuade you, that He who is said to have appeared to Abraham, and to Jacob, and to Moses, and who is called God, is distinct from Him who made all things, I mean numerically, not in will (Dialogue with Trypho, 56).*

From the above, we glean the following: Jesus, whom Justin calls the *Logos,* is not God Himself, but *next to God.* He, further, speculates that Jesus is *another God* who is subordinate to God. In addition, Justin calls Christ *an Angel.* Justin's fanciful and unbiblical speculations are, at best, not dignified with a comment, but because the majority of the Christian world believes in a distinction between God and His Word, we must address it briefly. That Christ the Word (*Logos*) and God are one and the same is something the Apostle John was careful to point out.

> ***John 1:1*** *In the beginning was the Word, and the Word was with God, and the Word was God.*
>
> ***John 1:2*** *The same was in the beginning with God.*
>
> ***John 1:3*** *All things were made by him; and without him was not any thing made that was made.*

The Greek-English Interlinear Bible reads, "…and God was the Word (John 1:1)[2]. Since God Himself is the Word, according to John, there is no room for speculating that Jesus is another, distinct God or Angel, as Justin postulates. Jesus Christ is the Word of God made flesh (John 1:14). What this simply means is that the same Word who walked with Adam and Eve in the Garden, revealed Himself as Word to Abraham, Moses, Samuel, and Nathan, among others, and created all things through this same Word, now was made flesh. If you were a contemporary of the Lord Jesus, and were privileged to touch His body, you would be touching the Word which created everything – you would be handling the creative, expressive identity of the Father, Himself. One man who experienced this privilege was John:

> ***1 John 1:1*** *That which was from the beginning, which we have heard, which we have seen with our eyes, which we have looked upon, and our hands have handled, of the Word of life;*

---

2 http://www.scripture4all.org/OnlineInterlinear/NTpdf/joh1.pdf

1 John 1:2 *(For the life was manifested, and we have seen it, and bear witness, and shew unto you that eternal life, which was with the Father, and was manifested unto us;)*

On the premise that the Word created everything, we can be assured that Jesus was no Angel, as Justin imagines. What is the difference between angels and God? It is the fact that angels are *created,* while God is not. Christ's body was not created, as Jehovah's Witnesses believe, but begotten of the Father. Justin's philosophy actually lessens and dishonors the identity of Jesus Christ, the one true God manifested in the flesh.

Many in the Christian world are unaware that there were serious arguments about doctrine, especially from the second century AD onwards. Why, for example, did the early Hellenistic (i.e. influenced by Greek philosophy) theologians feel pressured to make distinctions in the Godhead? In the Greek world, it was considered absurd to believe that God could suffer (in Latin *patripassianism* or literally the passion of God the Father). So, in order to gain acceptance among the gentile, Greek-influenced world, theologians, like

Justin, Tertullian, Origen, Athanasius, the Cappadocian fathers, and Augustine, to name a few, decided it was best not to identify Jesus with the Father. This is how the doctrine of the Word of God was transformed into something completely different and alien from what the Hebrew-speaking world believed.

What we must acknowledge, in accordance with the declaration of the Bible, is that Jesus Christ is not another God called the "Word of God" who lived together or beside the Father from eternity. John states "…God was the Word" (John 1:1). In the beginning, God and His Word were indistinguishable; when the Word was made flesh, God and His flesh, again, became one entity without divisions or distinctions. God created the world through His Word and now speaks to us through this very same Word.

> ***Hebrews 1:1*** *God, who at sundry times and in divers manners spake in time past unto the fathers by the prophets,*
>
> ***Hebrews 1:2*** *Hath in these last days spoken unto us by his Son, whom he hath appointed heir of all things, by whom also he made the worlds;*

The above Scriptures make it plain that God is not outside His flesh – His Son. In the days of the prophets, He appeared through His invisible Word; but in these last days, He is accessible only through His Word – Jesus Christ. This, in a nutshell, captures the essence of the Word made flesh (John 1:14). God is now to be acknowledged in Jesus Christ. To assign any other status, identity, or distinction to Jesus Christ is to challenge the claim of God. In fact, the Father refuses to talk to anyone, except through His flesh now.

> ***Luke 9:35*** *And there came a voice out of the cloud, saying, This is my beloved Son: hear him.*

The correct biblical image we are to conceive of is one God whose Spirit dwells in His own Heavenly flesh and blood now. It is for this reason that we cannot distinguish the suffering of the Father from the Son since the flesh belongs to the Father.

> ***Zechariah 12:10*** *And I will pour upon the house of David, and upon the inhabitants of Jerusalem, the spirit of grace and of supplications:*

> *and they shall look upon me whom they have pierced, and they shall mourn for him, as one mourneth for his only son, and shall be in bitterness for him, as one that is in bitterness for his firstborn.*

Notice that Jehovah, Himself, is speaking in Zechariah 12:10. He claims - centuries before the crucifixion - that the children of Israel will *look upon me whom they have pierced.* This can only mean that the suffering of the Father and Christ are the same. This verse disturbed Jehovah's Witnesses to such a degree that they took the liberty of changing Zechariah 12:10 to read…*they will see the one whom they have pierced* (New World Translation). The specific "I" of Jehovah, which identified Him with Jesus, now becomes the indefinite "the one" in the shocking theology of the Watchtower Society.

Understanding the doctrine of God and His Word being one and the same is not just an exercise in theological abstraction. There is a direct correlation with our understanding of the Word of God and our answers to prayer. The encounter between the Lord Jesus Christ and the Roman centurion is a classic example.

> ***Mathew 8:8*** *The centurion answered and said, Lord, I am not worthy that thou shouldest come under my roof: but speak the word only, and my servant shall be healed.*

> ***Matthew 8:9*** *For I am a man under authority, having soldiers under me: and I say to this man, Go, and he goeth; and to another, Come, and he cometh; and to my servant, Do this, and he doeth it.*

Somehow, the centurion understood that Jesus was the creative power of God. He was humbled by this profound knowledge, considering himself to be unworthy for the God manifested in flesh to enter his house, although he was a man of authority. *Speak thy word only and my servant shall be healed* tells us that he was well-acquainted with the manner in which the Word or *Dawbar* of Yahweh operated. The psalmist states:

> ***Psalm 107:20*** *He sent his word, and healed them, and delivered them from their destructions.*

> ***Psalm 147:15*** *He sendeth forth his commandment upon earth: his word runneth very swiftly.*

Perhaps the centurion, being the devout man of God that he was, concluded when he heard about the mighty works of Jesus, that this was the Word made flesh. Emboldened in this belief, he approached Jesus and revealed his understanding of the identity of the Lord. No wonder Jesus marveled and responded:

> ***Matthew 8:10*** *When Jesus heard it, he marvelled, and said to them that followed, Verily I say unto you, I have not found so great faith, no, not in Israel.*

Let us put Jesus' words into perspective. There were countless giants of faith in Israel but, according to Jesus, the Roman centurion – a gentile and colonizer – surpassed them. This is very impressive. Why was this case? It is, undoubtedly, because the centurion believed and declared Jesus to be identical with the creative Word of God which made all things, and was none other than the God of the Jews, something about which Jesus had a hard time convincing the Jews. In other words, a revelation of the identity of the Word of God impresses and moves God to bestow blessings upon us; this is praying with true understanding. No wonder the Psalmist rejoices at the sayings (Word) of God.

> ***Psalm 138:2*** *I bow myself toward Thy holy temple, And I confess Thy name, For Thy kindness, and for Thy truth, For Thou hast made great Thy saying above all Thy name (Young's Literal Translation).*

Why has God magnified His Word above all His name? One reason is because His name is dependent on His Word for revelation. Put differently, the only way we can know the wonderful name of Jesus, for example, is through a study of the inspired teaching of the Word of God. Without His Word, we cannot know His glorious name.

> ***John 5:39*** *Search the scriptures; for in them ye think ye have eternal life: and they are they which testify of me.*

I began this chapter by stressing that the Word of God is His expressive, creative power. It is significant that God chose to call Himself "The Word."

> **Revelation 19:13** *And he was clothed with vesture dipped in blood: and his name is called The Word of God.*

Why did He not choose to call Himself by some other designation or appellation – perhaps, "The thought of God?" I believe this is because God desires, above all, to communicate with us. "Word" refers to communication. Speech is a priceless gift given to humans, alone. Through words, we communicate ideas, visions, and truth. None of our civilizations would have been possible without the gift of the word – communication. What would human relations be without the ability to express hope, dreams, fears, compassion, and love?

How impoverished would our existence be without the innate capacity to learn to read and enjoy books? God Himself, I believe, rejoices when little children (and adults) begin to read and understand the written word because He gave us this capacity to communicate with Him through His written Word. Moses solemnly commanded the children of Israel:

Deuteronomy 6:6 *And these words, which I command thee this day, shall be in thine heart:*

Deuteronomy 6:7 *And thou shalt teach them diligently unto thy children, and shalt talk of them when thou sittest in thine house, and when thou walkest by the way, and when thou liest down, and when thou risest up.*

Too many Christians who wish to familiarize themselves with the God of the Bible make a mistake by going straight to the writings of people like Justin or Tertullian, rather than communicating directly with the Author of the Bible. Before one approaches the commentator, it would be more advisable to consult the Author Himself.

I once attended a theology seminar during my PhD studies in London, only to discover that the views of theologians, like Paul Tillich, Karl Rahner, Dietrich Bonhoeffer, and Rudolf Karl Bultmann were central to the discussion. Never once during the whole-day seminar was the Bible opened. The speculations of these men were elevated above the Word of God. The Author of the Bible is alive and well. Why do we treat Him like some long-dead author whose true meanings are buried with the past? There is a danger of teaching for doctrine the tradition of men (Matthew 15:9). Let us emulate the example of the Psalmist who was determined to praise God, in as much as he understood Him through His Word alone.

> ***Psalm 56:4*** *In God I will praise his word, in God I have put my trust; I will not fear what flesh can do unto me.*

Only one God can extend to us the gift of salvation because, like Creation, salvation is the prerogative of one God, alone. This doctrine is fleshed out in the next chapter.

3. GOD ALONE CAN SAVE

> ***Psalm 3:8*** *Salvation belongeth unto the Lord: thy blessing is upon thy people. Selah.*

To save is to deliver from the power of sin, sickness, the grave, and eternal death. This can only be the exclusive domain of God. As the psalmist, above, proclaims, "salvation belongeth unto the Lord…" Now, all professing Christians believe, and rightly so, that Jesus Christ died on the Cross of Calvary, shed His blood, and redeemed us from the curse of sin. However, they fail to understand that, if Jesus is not God the Father, then another God has saved us. This would contradict the Scripture, cited below, where the one God, Jehovah, claims to be the author of salvation.

> ***Hosea 13:14*** *I will ransom them from the power of the grave; I will redeem them from death: O death, I will be thy plagues; O grave, I will be thy destruction: repentance shall be hid from mine eyes.*

God uses the first personal pronoun, "I", four times. He emphatically declares that He will ransom us from the power of the grace, redeem us from death, plague death itself, and destroy the grave. How are we to understand this Scripture? Obviously, it means what it says – that Jehovah, Himself, will accomplish these acts of salvation. But is that what Christians believe today? The answer, regrettably, is no. They maintain that the second member of the Trinity, Jesus Christ - and, not God the Father – was commissioned to come down to earth and die for the sins of the world.

If the above is true, then we *cannot* praise the Father for personally bringing about our salvation. We shall have to praise the Son. This should leave Trinitarians in an uncomfortable position because it implies that the other two members of the Trinity – the Father and the Holy Spirit – where passively watching as the Son suffered and died. Thankfully, such a conception of salvation is not consistent with the Bible. As mentioned earlier, salvation is the domain or prerogative of the one God, alone, who repeatedly declares, "I will ransom…I will redeem…I will…." (Hosea 13:14).

The prophet Isaiah confirms that God was alone in the act of saving the world.

> ***Isaiah 59:16*** *And he saw that there was no man, and wondered that there was no intercessor: therefore his arm brought salvation unto him; and his righteousness, it sustained him.*

In the verse, above, Isaiah makes it clear that there was no collaborator with God in saving us. The truth is that God looked everywhere, but could not find anyone who met the criteria for saving mankind - let alone finding a savior, God could not even find an intercessor, or someone to stand in the gap and pray. So, what was God's final remedy? "Therefore His arm brought salvation unto him…" This cannot be any plainer – *His arm brought salvation unto Him.* This demonstrates that God is always the author and finisher of unique acts, such as Creation and salvation. In these spheres, we expect nothing less. If others can create and save, then this undermines the "omnipotence" of God. Significantly, Isaiah repeats this very same declaration just four chapters later.

Isaiah 63:5 *And I looked, and there was none to help; and I wondered that there was none to uphold: therefore mine own arm brought salvation unto me; and my fury, it upheld me.*

Could it be that God was preempting those who would declare that the second member of the Trinity, and not God the Father, was responsible for the act of salvation? Was this God's way of protesting His sovereignty over the domain of salvation? Notice in the verse, above, that God states…my *own* arm…The word, *own,* is not found in Isaiah 59:16, but this time God adds it as if to underscore His very own involvement in salvation.

Now, no one would dispute the fact that the Lord Jesus Christ is our Savior. But the core of the controversy, here, is whether Jesus is the *very same* God who spoke in Hosea 13:14, or distinct and, thus, not the same God. There is one powerful verse in the New Testament which has often surprised those who do not see that Jesus is the same God as the Father. This verse, uttered by a Jewish Rabbi, Paul, actually states that the blood of Jesus is the blood of God Himself:

> ***Act 20:28*** *Take heed therefore unto yourselves, and to all the flock, over the which the Holy Ghost hath made you overseers, to feed the church of God, which he hath purchased with his own blood.*

It is crystal clear that it was God who redeemed us with His very own blood. What we must understand is that the blood that ran in the veins and arteries of Jesus Christ is the blood of Jehovah, Himself. Furthermore, since life is in the blood, it follows that the life of Jesus Christ is the life of the Father Himself. After all, this was what Jesus continually declared to the Jews.

> ***John 6:57*** *As the living Father hath sent me, and I live by the Father: so he that eateth me, even he shall live by me.*

Think about it for a moment. If Jesus was not the Father manifested in flesh, where did He get the audacity to invite people to eat His flesh and drink His blood? This is not a side issue, for the Law of Moses makes the drinking of blood a very serious offense in the sight of God. There is a direct association between blood and life. To drink blood is to disrespect the sanctity of life, itself.

> ***Leviticus 17:11*** *For the life of the flesh is in the blood: and I have given it to you upon the altar to make an atonement for your souls: for it is the blood that maketh an atonement for the soul.*

Thankfully, for those who believe that Jesus Christ is the Father manifested in flesh, no such tensions exist. The same Father, who spoke in Hosea 13:14 & Isaiah 59:16, now comes with His own flesh and blood to fulfill the promise of effectuating salvation. The divine flesh and blood is the righteousness of God with which He clothed Himself:

> ***Isaiah 59:17*** *For he put on righteousness as a breastplate, and an helmet of salvation upon his head; and he put on the garments of vengeance for clothing, and was clad with zeal as a cloak.*

From Genesis to Revelation, the holy men and women of God constantly awaited His salvation which was renewed every so often. While waiting with expectation, they offered animal sacrifices every time they sinned. They looked to God, alone, to provide for their ultimate salvation and deliver them from the scourge of sin and a guilty conscience. They resigned themselves to wait for the salvation of Jehovah.

> ***Micah 7:7*** *Therefore I will look unto the Lord; I will wait for the God of my salvation: my God will hear me.*

> ***Lamentations 3:26*** *It is good that a man should both hope and quietly wait for the salvation of the Lord.*

With time, the children of Israel realized that the blood of goats and bulls does not deliver from sin. The daily sacrifices and offerings were only acceptable in so far as they pointed to the coming of the salvation of Jehovah – Jesus Christ, whose flesh and blood would make an eternal offering for sin.

> ***Hebrews 10:10*** *By the which will we are sanctified through the offering of the body of Jesus Christ once for all.*

Perhaps, those who maintain that the doctrine of the Trinity is essential for salvation are unaware of the true implications of what they promulgate. They tell us that God the Father is not the Son. Take a look at the figure, below, which represents

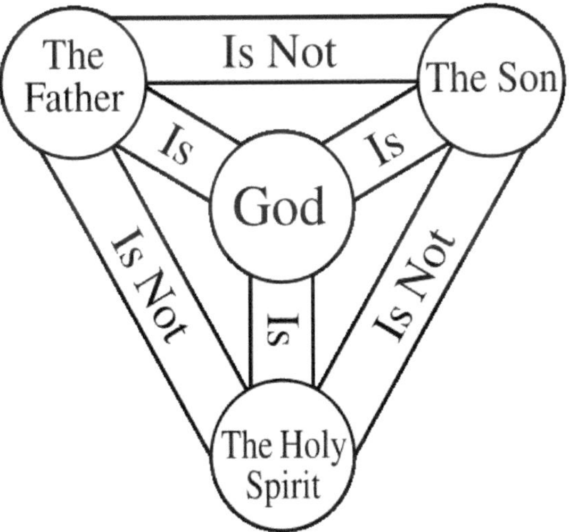

the classical understanding of the doctrine of the Trinity.

Now, it is plain to see that they do not consider the Father to be the Son, nor the Holy Spirit, and vice versa. With regards to salvation, this raises serious problems. For instance, the Apostle Peter, filled with the Spirit made this declaration to the ecclesiastical powers in Jerusalem:

> ***Act 4:12*** *Neither is there salvation in any other: for there is none other name under Heaven given among men, whereby we must be save.*

If we take the words of Peter seriously, it would mean that salvation does not belong to the Father and the Holy Spirit, since only the name of the Son, Jesus, can save us. Obviously, this is an absurd and unbiblical position. What, then, becomes of the declaration of Jehovah in Hosea 13:14 and Isaiah 59:16 & 63:5? The correct biblical position is that God brought about salvation through *His own arm* (Isaiah 63:5). God is using anthropomorphic language, which means that he is employing words which we humans can understand. What does He mean by *my own arm?* Think about your own arm. It is not a distinct or separate part of your body; it is connected to the rest of your anatomy through bones, tissue, muscle, blood, etc. If it were to be amputated, it would slowly dry up and waste away. Although God had no human arm to speak of when He spoke through Isaiah, He wanted us to think along the line I just described to help us better comprehend what He was going to do – robe Himself in His own flesh and blood. Take a careful look at the Scriptures, below:

> ***John 8:24*** *I said therefore unto you, that ye shall die in your sins: for if ye believe not that I am he, ye shall die in your sins.*
>
> ***John 8:25*** *Then said they unto him, Who art thou? And Jesus saith unto them, Even the same that I said unto you from the beginning.*
>
> ***John 8:26*** *I have many things to say and to judge of you: but he that sent me is true; and I speak to the world those things which I have heard of him.*
>
> ***John 8:27*** *They understood not that he spake to them of the Father.*

In the exchange, above, the Lord begins by saying that if they do not believe "that I am he," they would die in their sins. John 8:27 makes the connection: "They understood not that he spake to them of the Father." By declaring Himself to be the "I am," the Lord was revealing His identity as the Father, but His audience rejected this. I wonder how many read the words of Jesus everyday and fail to recognize that He is claiming to be the Father, Himself. I have learnt to be patient with seekers because even the Apostles, themselves, who were there when these conversations took place, harbored many doubts about the true identity of Jesus.

> ***John 14:7*** *If ye had known me, ye should have known my Father also: and from henceforth ye know him, and have seen him.*

> ***John 14:8*** *Philip saith unto him, Lord, shew us the Father, and it sufficeth us.*

> ***John 14:9*** *Jesus saith unto him, Have I been so long time with you, and yet hast thou not known me, Philip? he that hath seen me hath seen the Father; and how sayest thou then, Shew us the Father?*

There is no escaping the import of the words of Jesus. "From henceforth ye know him (i.e. the Father) and *have seen him*" (John 14:7). If one reads this and retains his or her composure, then, perhaps, they need to slowly reread it. In effect, the Lord states that after three years in His company, He expected them to know that He was the Father. Why was this necessary? The only reason is because only the Father reserves the right to save us, which explains why the Lord challenged their understanding of Him. In other words, it is not sufficient to merely believe that Jesus Christ is the Savior of the world, but equally important to believe that He is the one, indivisible God.

There is also a need to briefly address the belief of those who hold that the Lord came into this world in human flesh and blood, much like ours. It may come as a surprise to them to read that this is not supported by Scriptures. For example:

> ***Psalm 49:7*** *None of them can by any means redeem his brother, nor give to God a ransom for him:*
>
> ***Psalm 49:8*** *(For the redemption of their soul is precious, and it ceaseth for ever:)*

Humans of the race of Adam cannot hope to atone for the sin of humanity because our blood is collectively tainted by the sin of Adam and Eve. It is like someone with diseased blood attempting to give a blood transfusion to save someone else. In fact, this point should make us appreciate the statement in Isaiah 53:16 …*and he saw that there was no man*… We, humans, are tribal in the sense that we are prejudiced towards accepting only that with which we can relate and identify. So instead of accepting the biblical evidence that God came in His own Heavenly flesh and blood, some decided to "humanize" God and make Him "one of us." The Lord, however, claimed a Heavenly origin for His body, and Gabriel said much the same.

> ***John 8:23*** *And he said unto them, Ye are from beneath; I am from above: ye are of this world; I am not of this world.*

> ***Luke 1:35*** *And the angel answered and said unto her, The Holy Ghost shall come upon thee, and the power of the Highest shall overshadow thee: therefore also that holy thing which shall be born of thee shall be called the Son of God.*

It stands to reason that, if God came into this world, He must have a unique heavenly/divine aspect to His flesh and blood. His body must contain and epitomize all that which belongs to the Father. Significantly, the Lord never showed any solidarity with us humans in respect to our biological origins. God the Father, speaking 700 years before the Word was made flesh, declares:

> ***Isaiah 26:19*** *Thy dead men shall live, together with my dead body shall they arise. Awake and sing, ye that dwell in dust: for thy dew is as the dew of herbs, and the earth shall cast out the dead.*

The body of Christ is called "My dead body" by the Father. This furnishes us with a beautiful explanation of what was going on when the Lord ministered on the earth for 33 years. His body was begotten of the Holy Spirit, which we shall see later is the same as the Father, and God was in this body, saving sinners from the power sin.

> ***2 Corinthians 5:19*** *To wit, that God was in Christ, reconciling the world unto himself, not imputing their trespasses unto them; and hath committed unto us the word of reconciliation.*

There we have it in a nutshell! God was *in Christ.* This is contrary to what Trinitarians believe. They believe that the three members of the Trinity are beside each other, but Paul declares that God was in Christ. This will require a readjusting of positions, if you will. If God is in Christ, then we are speaking of one God, alone. Further to this, God, then, was not passively looking at Christ suffering, but He was experiencing all the pain and agony through His body. As it is written:

> ***Psalm 69:9*** *For the zeal of thine house hath eaten me up; and the reproaches of them that reproached thee are fallen upon me.*

This was not a shared agony between two individuals, but one and the same, with God experiencing the rejection, pain, misery, and reproaches through one body. Salvation is not a joint venture between three beings that operate consensually, but the work of one God.

> ***Hosea 13:4*** *Yet I am the Lord thy God from the land of Egypt, and thou shalt know no god but me: for there is no saviour beside me.*

> ***Titus 2:13*** *Looking for that blessed hope, and the glorious appearing of the great God and our Saviour Jesus Christ;*

Paul tells Titus that we are looking for the great God and our Savior Jesus Christ. Needless to say, there cannot be three great Gods any more than there can be three great Saviors.

Throughout this chapter, I have been making reference to Hosea 13:14 as conclusive evidence that God, alone, will redeem us from the grave. So, when was this fulfilled, and by whom? The Apostle Paul waxes lyrical when he makes the connection:

> ***1 Corinthians 15:54*** *So when this corruptible shall have put on incorruption, and this mortal shall have put on immortality, then shall be brought to pass the saying that is written, Death is swallowed up in victory.*
>
> ***1 Corinthians 15:55*** *O death, where is thy sting? O grave, where is thy victory?*
>
> ***1 Corinthians 15:56*** *The sting of death is sin; and the strength of sin is the law.*
>
> ***1 Corinthians 15:57*** *But thanks be to God, which giveth us the victory through our Lord Jesus Christ.*

Remember that God said, "I will redeem them…" in Hosea. If Christ fulfilled this prophecy, as we all agree, then Jesus is the very same Jehovah of the Old Testament, and not a distinct member of some diffuse committee.

In the remaining part of this chapter, I would like to insert excerpts from a sermon I preached, recently, which praises Jesus as the Savior from the womb to the tomb. It highlights events in the womb of Mary and the tomb of Joseph of Arimathea which show Jesus to, indeed, be the one Savior of mankind.

> ***Luke 1:41*** *And it came to pass, that, when Elisabeth heard the salutation of Mary, the babe leaped in her womb; and Elisabeth was filled with the Holy Ghost:*

The earthly life of our Lord and Saviour Jesus Christ was an active one from the womb to the tomb. Jesus is always Alpha and Omega, the beginning and the end, a fact which He proved during the 33 years of His earthly life. Let me show Jesus as the beginning - the Alpha of life first. He was not silent in the womb, but filled

Elisabeth with the Holy Ghost and filled baby John with joy before they could see Him. Jesus began His ministry in the womb because God cannot be silenced in the womb – He is not a human being who remains silent, helpless and ignorant for 9 months, shut up in darkness. John, although a baby, recognized the voice of His Creator and Savior, and leaped for joy in the womb.

If a six-month baby can respond to the voice of Jesus through Mary, surely we adults can do better. John was still a baby with no knowledge of the Torah, nor the difference between the theology of the Pharisees and the Sadducees, yet he leaped for joy at the sound of His God and Saviour. Some critics like to ask us, "How can you feel the joy of the Holy Ghost when you cannot see this God you are worshipping?" My answer to them is "Ask baby John." He could not see Jesus either, but he leapt for joy at the sound of the voice of Jesus. If God says, "Shalom," to you and me, it is reason enough to leap for joy. God extends His peace and blessing to us.

No human being has ever chosen whether he or she will be born, and certainly not where they will be born. Concerning Jesus, however, the Bible states:

> ***Micah 5:2*** *But thou, Bethlehem Ephratah, though thou be little among the thousands of Judah, yet out of thee shall he come forth unto me that is to be ruler in Israel; whose goings forth have been from of old, from everlasting.*

Not only did He choose the town where He would be born, but He also chose the womb through which He would enter the world. He sent Gabriel to make His "reservation." Now, Gabriel came to give understanding to Mary about whom it was who would soon be occupying her womb. I used to hear many preachers say that angels are forbidden to preach the Gospel. However, this is not entirely true. Notice what Gabriel says to Mary:

> **Luke 1:31** *And, behold, thou shalt conceive in thy womb, and bring forth a son, and shalt call his name Jesus.*

Luke 1:32 *He shall be great, and shall be called the Son of the Highest: and the Lord God shall give unto him the throne of his father David:*

Luke 1:33 *And he shall reign over the house of Jacob for ever; and of his kingdom there shall be no end.*

God wanted to make sure that Mary knew who it was who was seeking to "reserve" her womb. God has declared, "I am the Lord: that is my name: and my glory will I not give to another, neither my praise to graven images" (Isaiah 42:8). God wanted exclusive rights over her womb. He must be first in everything. He has the right; He is God, her Creator. To be the First, the Alpha, also means that He is given full control over that which He wishes to bless.

Then there is the tomb. Just as Jesus borrowed the womb of a woman, He now borrowed the tomb of a man, Joseph of Arimathaea. This was, again, something which no human had used before and had been prophesied by Isaiah 700 years before.

> ***John 19:41*** *Now in the place where he was crucified there was a garden; and in the garden a new sepulchre, wherein was never man yet laid.*

> ***John 19:42*** *There laid they Jesus therefore because of the Jews' preparation day; for the sepulchre was nigh at hand.*

> ***Isaiah 53:9*** *And he made his grave with the wicked, and with the rich in his death; because he had done no violence, neither [was any] deceit in his mouth.*

Was Jesus silent in the tomb? Absolutely not! Had the devil known beforehand the work of salvation Jesus would accomplish while in the tomb, he, perhaps, may not have allowed Him to be crucified. Jesus went to open the prison of those whom Satan held captive. He, now, led captivity captive:

> ***1 Peter 3:18*** *For Christ also hath once suffered for sins, the just for the unjust, that he might bring us to Gòd, being put to death in the flesh, but quickened by the Spirit:*

> **1 Peter 3:19** *By which also he went and preached unto the spirits in prison;*

Like the womb, an angel invited the weeping women to come in and see the place where Jesus lay:

> **Matthew 28:6** *He is not here: for he is risen, as he said. Come, see the place where the Lord lay.*

Do you know why the angel asked the disciples to go in and see the place where Jesus lay? This was not only for the obvious reason that His body was not there, but the fact that the linen clothes and napkin were separated, all wrapped up, and lying neatly in a corner, making it unlikely that thieves had come and stolen His body. What thief comes and robs a body, and then has the time to separate, fold, and wrap the linen coverings?

> **John 20:6** *Then cometh Simon Peter following him, and went into the sepulchre, and seeth the linen clothes lie,*

John 20:7 *And the napkin, that was about his head, not lying with the linen clothes, but wrapped together in a place by itself.*

John 20:8 *Then went in also that other disciple, which came first to the sepulchre, and he saw, and believed.*

In summary, the womb and the tomb demonstrate that Jesus is God of the beginning and the end. At a time when humans are helpless, He was God of both. He blessed and worked salvation from the womb and the tomb also. There is also a challenge that this sermon presents us with. God gave Mary and Joseph of Arimathaea the opportunity to give Him first priority and exclusive rights over the womb and the tomb. Fortunately, they understood that God requires us to voluntarily give Him the first-fruits. The God who asked for the first-fruits of the land and the firstborn son of every household of Israel now asked for the womb and the tomb. Let Him be the God of the womb and the tomb so He can bless us all. Indeed, God almighty has fulfilled His promise to save the world and destroy death through Jesus Christ. As the prophet said, He is lowly and humble, but having salvation:

> ***Zechariah 9:9*** *Rejoice greatly, O daughter of Zion; shout, O daughter of Jerusalem: behold, thy King cometh unto thee: he is just, and having salvation; lowly, and riding upon an ass, and upon a colt the foal of an ass.*

There is much confusion about the identity of the Holy Spirit in the denominational world. Some even believe the Holy Spirit to be an impersonal force. The next chapter will give biblical evidence to demonstrate that, since God is Spirit - that is, His essence; we cannot create a distinct identity for the Holy Spirit.

4. ONE GOD IS THE SPIRIT

Those who embrace the traditional doctrine of the Trinity believe in a literal distinction between the three "persons" of the Trinity. Often, this distinction leads to one person receiving less attention than the others. From their writings, we can discern that it is the person of the Holy Spirit which is frequently relegated to the margin. In his book with the telling title, *The Forgotten Trinity*, James R. White (1998) explains why, in his opinion, the Holy Spirit receives less attention than the Father and the Son.

> *There is a reason why the Holy Spirit does not receive the same kind of attention that is focused upon the Father and the Son: it is not His purpose to attract that kind of attention to himself...He does not seek to push himself into the forefront and gain attention for himself...One result of this voluntary role of the Spirit in the work of salvation is that the evidences of His*

personality and deity are not as numerous or obvious as those for the Father or the Son.[3]

There are several problems with such an explanation. To begin with, it raises a number of questions relating to the so-called co-equality of the three. According to James R. White, the Holy Spirit does not like to gain attention for Himself, unlike the Father and the Son, although he doesn't state the latter, it is clearly assumed. This is evidence that Trinitarians believe in three separate "Gods", as each one seems to have a different personality – where the first two "seek attention", while the third member seems more modest and is content to allow the first two to share the limelight. White confesses that there aren't many Scriptures which clearly prove the personality of the Holy Spirit. The truth is that there are no Scriptures to support such a polytheistic

---

3

White, J. (1998). *The Forgotten Trinity: Recovering the heart of Christian belief.* Minnesota: Bethany House Publishers. Page 139.

conception of the Godhead. To gain a biblical understanding of the identity of the Holy Spirit, we will need to start in the beginning:

> **Genesis 1:1** *In the beginning God created the Heaven and the earth.*

> **Genesis 1:2** *And the earth was without form, and void; and darkness was upon the face of the deep. And the Spirit of God moved upon the face of the waters.*

When God created the Heavens and the earth, His Spirit *moved* on the face of the waters. Earlier, we saw how the one God created all things. Genesis 1:2 shows that the Creation was set in motion when the Spirit of God moved. We can only conclude that the Spirit of God is His very own essence. In order to create *ex nihilo* (out of nothing), renew, refresh, and sustain, among others, the Spirit of God – i.e. He, Himself – must move and act.

> **Psalm 104:30** *Thou sendest forth thy spirit, they are created: and thou renewest the face of the earth.*

Another way to comprehend this is to ask the following question with some caution: what is God? The answer is Spirit, as Jesus, Himself, teaches us.

> ***John 4:24*** *God is a Spirit: and they that worship him must worship him in spirit and in truth.*

In John 4:24, Jesus makes no distinction between God and the Spirit. When one prays in the Spirit, one is praying to God. To envision God is to envision a spiritual being; to approach Him is to seek communication with Him through His Spirit. God and His Spirit are one and the same. The titles God the Father, and the Holy Spirit highlight different functions of the same God, but refer to the same being. That the father and the Holy Spirit, are the same, can easily be verified in the Scriptures if we ask the question: who begat the son? Have a look at the two verses below:

> ***Matthew 1:20*** *But while he thought on these things, behold, the angel of the Lord appeared unto him in a dream, saying, Joseph, thou son of David, fear not to take unto thee Mary thy wife: for that which is conceived in her is of the Holy Ghost.*

> ***John 3:16*** *For God so loved the world, that he gave his only begotten Son, that whosoever believeth in him should not perish, but have everlasting life.*

On the surface, the two verses seem to contradict each other: Mathew 1:20 states that the Holy Spirit gave birth to the Son, while John 3:16 claims God gave birth to the Son. This is not a problem for one God adherents: God the Father is identical with the Holy Spirit. The two titles are often used interchangeably in the Bible. Take the two verses that follow as cases in point:

> ***Act 5:3*** *But Peter said, Ananias, why hath Satan filled thine heart to lie to the Holy Ghost, and to keep back part of the price of the land?*

> ***Act 5:4*** *Whiles it remained, was it not thine own? and after it was sold, was it not in thine own power? why hast thou conceived this thing in thine heart? thou hast not lied unto men, but unto God.*

Peter accused Ananias of lying to the Holy Ghost in verse 3, only to declare that he had lied to God in verse 4. It would not make any sense whatsoever to maintain that the Holy Spirit does not seek to gain attention for Himself; if the Holy Spirit is God, which He is, then He must be glorified and magnified as such. After all, it is a command to do so:

> ***Matthew 4:10*** *Then saith Jesus unto him, Get thee hence, Satan: for it is written, Thou shalt worship the Lord thy God, and him only shalt thou serve.*

This booklet affirms the cornerstone teaching that the God of the Bible is indivisibly one, and to believe this is a matter of salvation. With reference to the identity of the Holy Spirit, a good place to begin is the Scripture, below:

> ***Ephesians 4:4*** *There is one body, and one Spirit, even as ye are called in one hope of your calling;*

Now, most Christians will readily concede that there, indeed, is but one Spirit. The bone of contention, however, is whether this one Spirit is the same Spirit that dwelt in, and was the life, of the Son of God (John 6:57). In this matter, one God Christians part ways with Trinitarians. The latter believe that the Holy Spirit is not the Son (remember the figure?). The Scriptures are not silent on this issue. Speaking about the veil which Christ shall take away, the Apostle Paul identifies Jesus as the Spirit of God.

> ***2 Cor 3:14*** *But their minds were blinded: for until this day remaineth the same vail untaken away in the reading of the old testament; which vail is done away in Christ.*
> ***2 Cor 3:15*** *But even unto this day, when Moses is read, the vail is upon their heart*
> ***2 Cor 3:16*** *Nevertheless when it shall turn to the Lord, the vail shall be taken away*
> ***2 Cor 3:17*** *Now the Lord is that Spirit: and where the Spirit of the Lord is, there is liberty.*

Only God can fill us with His Holy Spirit. Only He can pour out of His essence into whosoever He chooses. After all, receiving the Holy Spirit is no different from God dwelling in us – Immanuel. In the Old Testament, the prophets of old frequently prophesied that God desired to pour out His Spirit upon all flesh.

> ***Joel 2:28*** *And it shall come to pass afterward, that I will pour out my spirit upon all flesh; and your sons and your daughters shall prophesy, your*

> *old men shall dream dreams, your young men shall see visions:*

Again, note the "I" of God. By this, we are to understand that it is His undertaking; His sovereign act alone. Remarkably, when the time for the fulfillment of this prophecy came, we are told in plain language that Jesus is the one who sent the Holy Ghost.

> **Matthew 3:11** *I indeed baptize you with water unto repentance: but he that cometh after me is mightier than I, whose shoes I am not worthy to bear: he shall baptize you with the Holy Ghost, and with fire:*

> **Luke 24:49** *And, behold, I send the promise of my Father upon you: but tarry ye in the city of Jerusalem, until ye be endued with power from on high.*

We are compelled to conclude that the one God speaking in Joel 2:28, and the Lord Jesus Christ, are one and the same. We are not to understand the "sending of the Holy Ghost" as if the Father sends the third member of a Trinity to fill believers. I fail to see how Trinitarians can hold such a position. How can one God "send" another God? The biblical account agrees with the understanding that one God, who is now manifested in the flesh, sends His own essence – His Spirit – to fill believers. This is why we receive the "Spirit of Christ."

> ***Romans 8:9*** *But ye are not in the flesh, but in the Spirit, if so be that the Spirit of God dwell in you. Now if any man have not the Spirit of Christ, he is none of his.*

Our objective is not to poke fun at those who envision three persons in the Godhead. This booklet, hopefully, will serve to challenge the taken-for-granted understanding of this very important doctrine of God. Apollos is described as "an eloquent man, and mighty in the Scriptures (Acts 18:24), but he was humble enough to be instructed by Aquila and Priscilla. I am convinced that the Lord is seeking out many Trinitarians to give them this wonderful and saving doctrine of the one God manifested in flesh, which the Apostles preached. I have found the verse, below, to be a powerful argument showing that the Spirit of Jesus Christ is the Holy Spirit.

> ***Galatians4:6*** *And because ye are sons, God hath sent forth the Spirit of his Son into your hearts, crying, Abba, Father.*

Many believe that they have received “another” Spirit, and not that of the Son of God, Jesus Christ. They believe this because they have misunderstood the words of Jesus:

> ***John 14:16*** *And I will pray the Father, and he shall give you another Comforter, that he may abide with you for ever;*

If they would only read the next verse, it would be abundantly clear that Jesus was speaking of the Spirit in Him, and not about a different, distinct third member of the Trinity. In fact, this is conclusively settled by verses 17 and 18.

> ***John 14:17*** *Even the Spirit of truth; whom the world cannot receive, because it seeth him not, neither knoweth him: but ye know him; for he dwelleth with you, and shall be in you.*

> ***John 14:18*** *I will not leave you comfortless: I will come to you.*

Who did the Apostles know except Jesus? Who was dwelling with the Apostles all this time, if not the Lord, Himself? Thankfully, the Lord put an end to any speculation by declaring, "I will not leave you comfortless: I will come to you." Could He have been any clearer? It is vital to appreciate that the Lord was eager to baptize them all with the Holy Spirit because, as long as He was with them in the flesh, they would be limited. As creatures that are sight-oriented, they would have remained passive, and deferred to the Lord at every instance. The spiritual principles of the Kingdom, however, operate on the basis of faith, and not sight.

> ***John 20:29*** *Jesus saith unto him, Thomas, because thou hast seen me, thou hast believed: blessed are they that have not seen, and yet have believed.*

It was necessary for the Lord to depart in flesh because it is the Spirit – His true essence – which is spatially limitless or omnipresent. Believers in any corner of the world can now assemble and experience the Spirit of the Lord Jesus Christ fellowshipping and ministering to them. This is what the Lord meant when He stated:

> ***Matthew 18:20*** *For where two or three are gathered together in my name, there am I in the midst of them.*

How did the early Christians perceive the status or identity of the Holy Spirit? When they prayed, how did they perceive the dynamics and blessings which came through the Spirit? Several Scriptures demonstrate that they believed they were receiving impartation from the Spirit of Jesus Christ, Himself, and not the Spirit as a distinct member.

> ***Philippians 1:19*** *For I know that this shall turn to my salvation through your prayer, and the supply of the Spirit of Jesus Christ,*

In all seriousness, it is patently absurd to believe that the Holy Spirit is God and, simultaneously, unwilling to "gain attention for himself," as James R. White opines:

> *He [Holy Spirit] is not "up front" and is not spoken of as often as the other persons. Some take this as evidence of inferiority, but as we have noted before, difference in function does not*

indicate inferiority of nature (White, 1998, p. 139).

All this effort at elevating the status of the Holy Spirit would have been unnecessary if White understood the one God doctrine. Those who deny the words of the *Shema Israel,* found in Deuteronomy 6:4, seem condemned to labor in vain with bizarre speculations to convince us and themselves that God is not one. Significantly, when Jesus declared the commandment in Deuteronomy 6:4 to be the first and most important one, the Jewish scribe declared this God to be *he* (singular):

> ***Mark 12:32*** *And the scribe said unto him, Well, Master, thou hast said the truth: for there is one God; and there is none other but he:*

In the final chapter, we will consider Scriptures that prove one God, alone, shall return. Furthermore, this same one God – Jesus Christ – will reign on the one throne in Heaven.

5. ONE GOD RETURNS

Whenever the prophets of God were given the privilege of peering into the very throne room of God in Heaven, they ascertained that there was only one throne, and one God sitting on it.

> ***1 Kings 22:19*** *And he said, Hear thou therefore the word of the Lord: I saw the Lord sitting on his throne, and all the host of Heaven standing by him on his right hand and on his left.*

"*The* Lord sitting on *his* throne" leaves no room for a Trinity reigning in Heaven. The picture has always been consistent: one God sitting on one throne surrounded by the host of Heaven. That which the Scriptures proclaim has been verified over and over again by the servants of the Lord. The prophet Isaiah confirms what Micaiah saw:

> ***Isaiah 6:1*** *In the year that king Uzziah died I saw also the Lord sitting upon a throne, high and lifted up, and his train filled the temple.*

The language is once again quintessentially one God – "*the* Lord sitting upon *a* throne... *his* train…" Why, may we ask, is there no sighting anywhere in the pages of the Bible of a Trinity of distinct persons? The truths of Heaven have always had witnesses who proclaimed what they saw. God, Himself, charges such witnesses to declare His identity as the one God who dwells by Himself.

> ***Isaiah 43:10*** *Ye are my witnesses, saith the Lord, and my servant whom I have chosen: that ye may know and believe me, and understand that I am he: before me there was no God formed, neither shall there be after me.*
> ***Isaiah 43:11*** *I, even I, am the Lord; and beside me there is no savior.*
> ***Isaiah 43:12*** *I have declared, and have saved, and I have shewed, when there was no strange god among you: therefore ye are my witnesses, saith the Lord, that I am God.*

Throughout the Old Testament, the Spirit of the Lord inspired the prophets to declare that one God would be revealing Himself in flesh. The same God who reigned, sitting on one throne in Heaven, would be manifested in the flesh. For some reason, no one was paying attention. Malachi specifically informs the children of Israel that the same God whom they worshipped and sought would suddenly come to the Temple.

> ***Malachi 3:1*** *Behold, I will send my messenger, and he shall prepare the way before me: and the Lord, whom ye seek, shall suddenly come to his temple, even the messenger of the covenant, whom ye delight in: behold, he shall come, saith the Lord of hosts.*

Who can be the Lord of *his* Temple except the one God, Jehovah? Indeed, the God of the Temple, whom devout Jews sought, suddenly appeared in the Temple in Jerusalem, but many were caught unawares. Some were found to be engaging in all manner of unholy business in His Temple. Note that Jesus calls the Temple "My house."

> ***Matthew 21:13*** *And said unto them, It is written, My house shall be called the house of prayer; but ye have made it a den of thieves.*

I have cause to fear that many will be caught unprepared when the Lord appears again. Not only unbelievers, but those who expect a triune God to appear will be ashamed. A well-known evangelist publicly declared that he saw a vision of the three persons of the Godhead descending to the earth. Clearly, such a vision is not grounded in the Bible at all. Zechariah boldly declares to us who live in the end times:

> ***Zechariah 14:9*** *And the Lord shall be king over all the earth: in that day shall there be one Lord, and his name one.*

Obviously, if one God shall return and have one name, this negates the doctrine of the Trinity. It would make no sense, and do no justice, to the three persons to be called by one name. It would be a very poor excuse to respond that the Father and the Holy Spirit will not seek to "gain attention for themselves," as James R. White would probably rationalize. How many Gods did Enoch preach would return to judge the world?

> ***Judge 1:14*** *And Enoch also, the seventh from Adam, prophesied of these, saying, Behold, the Lord cometh with ten thousands of his saints,*

The doctrine of how many Gods shall return will decisively prove how many Gods exist. The first time the one God entered this world, many stumbled and were offended. The paradox is that they read the same Bible and believed the same doctrine as the rest of Israel. But when they read Isaiah 9:6, for example, they could not accept that Jehovah would enter this world with a body.

> ***Isaiah 9:6*** *For unto us a child is born, unto us a son is given: and the government shall be upon his shoulder: and his name shall be called Wonderful, Counsellor, The mighty God, The everlasting Father, The Prince of Peace.*

I have often wondered why these devout Jews stumbled at so beautiful a prophecy. They read it for years and considered it to be a part of the inspired corpus of Scripture and yet, when the fullness of time came, their faith failed them. Today, too, I am afraid that those who quote from the same Bible as we do, attend church regularly, and expect the return of the Lord, will find themselves surprised that one God returns, *alone.*

> ***Revelation 19:11*** *And I saw Heaven opened, and behold a white horse; and he that sat upon him was called Faithful and True, and in righteousness he doth judge and make war.*

> ***Revelation 19:13*** *And he was clothed with a vesture dipped in blood: and his name is called The Word of God.*

In the *parousia* (second coming of Christ), John records seeing one God returning, mounted on a white horse. This God has a title, "The Word of God." Bible students will have no problem identifying Him as Jesus Christ (John 1.1, 14). We have seen, earlier, that the Scriptures decree the return of one God, alone (Zechariah 14:9). This fact is also reinforced by other Scriptures, such as the one below:

> ***Titus 2:13*** *Looking for that blessed hope, and the glorious appearing of the great God and our Saviour Jesus Christ;*

The Bible is replete with Scriptures exhorting believers to expect the return of but one God – Jesus Christ. It is of utmost importance that Paul calls Jesus "the great God and Saviour." The definite article, "the," highlights this fact. To expect the return of Jesus, alone, is to profess faith in the one God doctrine – The Father, Son and Holy Spirit are referring to the same God.

This was, indeed, the understanding of the Apostle Paul.

> ***Colossians 2:9*** *For in him dwelleth all the fulness of the Godhead bodily.*

When Christ returns, the Father, who is Spirit, will be found dwelling in the Son, and not outside of Him. To look at Jesus will be to look at the Father (John 14:9). To receive Jesus will be to receive the Father, who is the Holy Spirit.

> ***John 5:23*** *That all men should honour the Son, even as they honour the Father. He that honoureth not the Son honoureth not the Father which hath sent him.*

> ***1 John 2:23*** *Whosoever denieth the Son, the same hath not the Father: but he that acknowledgeth the Son hath the Father also.*

According to John, what one does with the Son will be considered as done to the Father. This rules out any distinctions between them. By way of example, if one prays to Jesus, one has prayed to the Father because He is not outside of Christ (2 Corinthians 5:19). Recall that the voice from Heaven said, "Hear ye him" (Matthew 17:5). The spotlight of Heaven and earth will be focused on Jesus Christ, alone, when He returns. Jesus is the name of the one God, who is Spirit and flesh in one. When every enemy will be conquered at the end of age, everything that breathes will bow down in surrender to one name – Jesus.

> ***Philippians 2:10*** *That at the name of Jesus every knee should bow, of things in Heaven, and things in earth, and things under the earth;*

The verse, above, is often cited in many churches all over the world; but few pause to reflect that it is a powerful witness to the one God doctrine. Paul, we must keep in mind, was a rabbi immersed in the Law and the prophets (*Tanakh*). He was citing a verse from the Old Testament in which Jehovah was speaking about the consummation of the age (parousia).

> ***Isaiah 45:23*** *I have sworn by myself, the word is gone out of my mouth in righteousness, and shall not return, That unto me every knee shall bow, every tongue shall swear.*

"That unto me" is proof positive that Jehovah and Jesus point to the same God. Although not something I normally recommend, it is of more than passing interest that individuals who have an NDE (near-death-experience) return back to life to speak about encountering one God, who sits on one throne, with an indescribably beautiful and powerful light emanating from His being. When the beloved Apostle, John, was invited to come up to Heaven, he, too, witnessed seeing one throne and one God sitting upon it.

> ***Revelation 4:1*** *After this I looked, and, behold, a door was opened in Heaven: and the first voice which I heard was as it were of a trumpet talking with me; which said, Come up hither, and I will shew thee things which must be hereafter.*

> ***Revelation 4:2*** *And immediately I was in the spirit: and, behold, a throne was set in Heaven, and one sat on the throne.*

At this juncture, I would like to interject my own testimony for the benefit of those who have not heard it before and, of course, for the glory of the Lord Jesus Christ. I come from a Muslim background; a Somali born in Jeddah, Saudi

Arabia. When I was eight years of age, I was sent to a boarding school in Nasik, India, where I completed my secondary education in 1988. In 1986, hungry for an experience with God, I prayed fervently, asking Him to reveal Himself. Barely three months later, I had a life-changing encounter which has defined my life ever since. One night, I awoke with the intention of going to the lavatory. To my horror, I looked back and saw my body lying on the bed, while I was floating above it in the air.

With a mighty surge, I was lifted up towards the sky and found myself standing above the clouds, which stretched evenly in every direction; the clouds were shot through with an orange-red tinge. Now this was no dream; in dreams, one often does not question the irrationality of events: in a flash you could change locations from Japan to the USA, with no questions asked. In my out-of-body-experience, I panicked, refused to accept that the Law of gravity was suspended, and tortured myself with questions of a scientific nature beyond the capacity of my poor brain to process.

Lo and behold, I saw a man standing quietly all along – like He has always been there – just fixedly staring at me. I instantly knew that this was Jesus, and that was settled beyond doubt. People often ask, "How do you know that it was Jesus?" I find this a curious question because one just knows "up there." There is something about that other world where you just know with a deep, profound knowledge. Perhaps, the Apostle Paul's words capture this sentiment best:

> ***1 Corinthians 13:12*** *For now we see through a glass, darkly; but then face to face: now I know in part; but then shall I know even as also I am known.*

Jesus called me to His side, put His arms around my shoulder, and walked up and down the length of the clouds for what seemed an eternity with me. All the while He spoke in a language which I have yet to hear spoken in this world. It was a Heavenly language which just edified me with every utterance. Later, when I awoke, I was disappointed to discover that I could not recollect a word in English. The Bible tells us that there is a new language in Heaven. In fact, this is one reason I believe in speaking in tongues because God's language is of a different order, if you will, a fact corroborated by Scripture:

> ***Zephaniah 3:9*** *For then will I turn to the people a pure language, that they may all call upon the name of the Lord, to serve him with one consent.*

When I awoke, my life was transformed instantaneously. What is truly astounding is that no one preached to me. Although I tried to tell myself that I just had an innocent dream, and could not possibly have met Jesus (which would mean I have to become a Christian), I found my manners, attitude and whole life was changing for the better. I could no longer use filthy language, a common behavior in our school, I found an abiding peace I could not deny, and I found myself asking for and devouring a Gideon's New Testament, given to me by, strangely, a Hindu friend.

I saw Jesus, alone. In the encounter, I knew He was God before He told me so Himself. The power, love, meekness, and majesty that emanated from Him could only belong to God. One reason

I adopted the name of Paul was because I identified with His experience on the Road to Damascus, where he met the one true God – Jesus Christ – and was profoundly transformed.

> **Act 9:5** *And he said, Who art thou, Lord? And the Lord said, I am Jesus whom thou persecutest: it is hard for thee to kick against the pricks.*

When one is as privileged as I was to see the Lord, I understand that He expects me to be a witness of what I saw. My experience aligns with that of countless others in the Bible. When the veil of this life is pulled back and the contending voices of this world subside, we shall come face to face with one God, seated on one throne. In my encounter with the Lord, He ordained that I should meet Him on the clouds. But, soon, He will come with the clouds to reign on earth. Are you prepared to meet Him?

> **Revelation 1:7** *Behold, he cometh with clouds; and every eye shall see him, and they also which pierced him: and all kindreds of the earth shall wail because of him. Even so, Amen.*

About the author

Paul Thomas is a doctoral student at King's College, London (Education). He is a minister in the Apostolic Church International Fellowship, Europe.

I would love to hear from you. Please feel free to correspond with me using the email below:

hpaulsilas@hotmail.com

Numbers 6:24 *The Lord bless thee, and keep thee:*
Numbers 6:25 *The Lord make his face shine upon thee, and be gracious unto thee:*
Numbers 6:26 *The Lord lift up his countenance upon thee, and give thee peace.*

www.ingramcontent.com/pod-product-compliance
Ingram Content Group UK Ltd.
Pitfield, Milton Keynes, MK11 3LW, UK
UKHW020219250726
13967UKWH00001B/91

9 781471 750991